W9-DDT-451

Your
GAMEPLAN

Build a Life
beyond
Survival Mode

Sarah Harnisch
Young Living Platinum

Jamine Deal
Young Living Ind. Distributor #3390472
jaminedeal@gmail.com
507-381-0712
www.YoungLiving.com

Your Gameplan

Layout and cover design: Jeremy Holden (JeremyHolden.me)

Editing team: Maria Waddell, Kat Hannah, and Trina Holden

CONTENTS

I loved my current job, was feeling pretty secure, made good money — until I was introduced to the Young Living business opportunity. It was hearing the words, "Why work so hard for someone else when you could be working that hard for yourself?" That was my "ah-ha" moment.

Shenatel Busby

I have more freedom and can make my family more of a priority!

Kimberly Esposito

I wondered if Young Living would really work... I laugh at that now. I almost don't recognize my life. We now have a residual income, the ability to travel, we've survived six months of my husband being un-employed, we've made many new friends, and I love that I am helping people have a better life. I love the products and use them every day. I love the people I get to interact with, they are some of the most amazing people in the world. I love that this extra income has allowed us to give abundantly to help the extreme poor and take a missions trip to Nicaragua.

Joy Hinterkopf

You Need a Gameplan

Are you tired?

Are you depleted in every possible way, and financially broken? With no time to fix it?

You don't see a way out. You have no hope. You have been living life this way for years.

You want more time with your kids. You desperately need to get away with your spouse. You want deeper friendships, people who have your back, but you have no time to invest in those friendships.

You want to take better care of your body, but that requires money. It requires resources to exercise the way you want and cook the way you should be cooking. But you are empty. You have been empty for a long time.

Perhaps you have a great job. You're doing what you believe you were called and created to do—but you have no time. You are worn from the nine-to-five grind. You would give just about anything to be free of your alarm clock. You feel trapped by the hours, or the pace, or the stress of your job. You don't see a way out. You have very little tucked away, and retirement is fast approaching. Or you're on the other end — just starting out, in college, or a high school graduate. You have no idea what's next. You have no Gameplan.

Maybe you are a mom or a dad who has chosen to stay home with your kids. Your spouse is working full time. You even have a part-time job in off hours, but it just isn't enough. You're in survival mode every single month. You live paycheck to paycheck. You get a little saved away and it's gone in the next crisis, as if months of saving never happened.

What if I told you there was a way out?

What if, in one little book, I could pour sunshine on your face? If I could give you hope that there is a future beyond where you are right now?

What if I told you that my entire world has been turned upside down in the past two years by getting out of the 40-hour work week, and I believe it's completely possible for ANYONE?

I believe it's possible if you are shy, if you have no friends, live in the middle of nowhere, and have no resources! Not only that... but what if I told you I wrote an entire book that shows you, step by step, in tiny bite-sized pieces, exactly what to do to break free? That book is called Gameplan. The book you have in your hands is a sample of it, to show you where this goes.

Where do you begin?

Start small.

Start with this tiny book in your hands. It is a quick read that offers some strategy and a lot of food for thought. Let the words melt in your mind and allow yourself to dream big. Walk with me for a bit.

Lose yourself in the possibility of freedom.

I'm going to tell you how I started a small business while homeschooling five kids, anchoring news 40 hours a week starting at 4 a.m. I began every day at the brink of exhaustion.

I've been where you are. I know that place of slavery. I know the weariness. I know the frustration of never getting ahead, decade after decade. I know that place so deeply that there are still days I wake up and have to remind myself that I am no longer there. It's like it was yesterday. I was there, but I dug out of it. And now my goal is to show as many people how to do it as possible — whether there is a benefit to me or not. It's not about the benefit. Sometimes, it's just about loving people. It's about having compassion when they need a leg up. I have nothing to gain or lose from you checking out the next two chapters of this book. But if you read it and move forward, you have everything to gain.

My name is Sarah, and this is my husband John. And this is the story of our Young Living home business. All you need to follow along is a dash of hope and an hour of free time.

Here is your task while reading these few pages: I want you to stack what I'm telling you against what you are doing right now. Weigh it side by side: a small business, run from your home, without a boss, without an alarm clock, on your time schedule — versus how you spend your time at work. See if your time can be used more effectively to pay off your debt, enjoy your family, work on your health, and grow time economy — the greatest wealth there is.

You need a change. You need a new gameplan.

This is it.

When I started my Young Living business I definitely wondered if I had what it takes. Was I good enough to do something like this? But I've had nothing but support from upline, downline and crossline. If I had to choose the BEST thing about having a Young Living business...The people. Every. Single. Person. That I have encountered so far with this business is unique and a blessing to the business in their own way. It's an amazing group of people as a whole.

Kayla Wileman

One of my favorite things about being a part of Young Living is the chance to help people. I am so thankful for how my family has been blessed through Young Living, but I am not satisfied to just see my family benefit. I believe that once we know there is a better way, we are called to share it. We are not blessed merely for the sake of being blessed, but we are blessed to be a blessing. That is what Young Living is to me. An avenue to bless others with a way to live above the line of wellness, to improve their way of living, and to help them find a way to do more than "just get by" financially. I love seeing people do well in life!

Sarah Hackett

SARAH'S STORY

To see why I'm so passionate about leading others to financial freedom, you have to understand a bit about where I came from. As you read, you will begin to see that your past does not have to define you, but can be the fuel that drives you to succeed.

A ROUGH START

I grew up in a suburban Chicago townhouse, in a poor family. My father was an alcoholic and car mechanic, and my mother pretty much raised my three siblings and me single-handedly. My dad has been in more DUI crashes than I can count, is a convicted felon, and has lost his driver's license for life.

The abuse was hard. I was the oldest; when the yelling got bad, I'd take my siblings into my bedroom and we'd have Amy Grant concerts, singing into a plastic ice cream cone as a microphone and cranking up the music so we could not hear. Many times I remember my mom waking us up, putting us in the car, and driving away; I wasn't sure if I'd see my dad again. Once, when I was in 4th grade, we stayed away for a full six months, living with my grandparents and aunt, and I had to enroll in a different school. But we always returned.

The neighborhood we lived in wasn't the greatest, either. Our subdivision was the drug trading ground for two gangs on either side of us.

I remember coming home from school one day to a drug raid going on in our subdivision. We had to sit there on the bus for 45 minutes as a helicopter flew overhead and SWAT teams entered the house.

I became engaged to my husband John when I was 16 years old and we were married three years later. For the first ten years of our marriage, we had babies every two years, while holding down four minimum wage jobs and full-time college courses. We lived off student loans, racking up $70,000 in debt.

The first year of our marriage, John worked eight hours a day for minimum wage at a gas station. He also worked another full-time job at a competing gas station across the street, eight hours on the overnight shift. He'd leave for one shift at 7 a.m., work until 5 p.m., come home and sleep four hours, and then go work another eight hour shift overnight. Then he would repeat it.

I typed addresses eight hours a day for a book publishing company (it's still the least favorite job I've ever had) and worked part-time for a Christian bookstore at night. I had a 21-hour course load in college night classes and was pregnant with our first son. That was our first year of marriage.

BELOW THE POVERTY LINE

Just about every month, we got an eviction notice. Even with four jobs, we could not maintain our rental, so we moved in with my parents and hunkered down for three years. Then we lived in government housing in Dixon, Illinois, and then in government housing in DeKalb, Illinois.

We were on public aid for everything: our medical card, LIHEAP heating assistance, the LINK food card, three food pantries, WIC food, government housing assistance, and gas cards through our church. Even with four jobs, we were still getting disconnect notices. When you make $5/hour, it's really hard to make an $800/month rent. We physically could not take on more than four jobs between us. For a 12-year period we lived in extreme poverty; balancing full-time college coursework with multiple jobs, toddlers, and nursing. During that time, I had 11 different jobs in the world of food service, until I caused the evacuation of a restaurant after setting a microwave on fire. Twice. (Food was not my niche!) Amidst all of that, I was prompted by a friend to apply for a job at a local radio station. I was hired there to work every other Saturday for three hour shifts at $4/hour. My first month's check was $21 after taxes. (I kept my day job!)

John and I adjusted to poverty, even while I was entering the world of radio. At the first government housing projects where we lived in Dixon, there were "water bugs" (cockroaches) crawling on the floors. We had almost no furniture, and the kids slept on mattresses on the floor because we could not afford beds for them.

FEASTING FROM THE FOOD PANTRY

We went through the transmissions in four used cars in six months. We'd go a few days with no food in the house; digging for a quarter to get a loaf of bread so the kids could eat, while John and I went hungry. We'd literally not have a morsel of food in the house, because when you have to choose between food or gas in your car to get to work, you pick the gasoline. I remember running out of meat for two weeks, waiting for the next food pantry to open. When I arrived, they were out of meat also, but had plenty of chocolate pudding. So we ate chocolate pudding for a couple of days until our next food card went through.

We lived from food pantry to food pantry. We had more eviction notices and utility disconnect warnings then I can count, but the Lord always came through. A check from a relative would come within hours of our power being shut off. We'd use birthday card money to stave off eviction. After a few years of college and a few years in radio at a tiny station in a trailer in a corn field, I was offered a job in downtown Chicago anchoring news for an all-news station. It had an audience of seven million people. I thought I had arrived! My income was $35,000 a year!

What I didn't count on was that taxes, gas to drive 72 miles one-way into work each day, tolls, and parking in Chicago took half my paycheck. Our family of seven was living off $16,000 a year, and still on food stamps. I was on the air with personalities who were making millions of dollars a year, and we didn't have enough food for our children.

We had done it right. John worked full-time and put me through college. I worked full-time and put him through college. We both graduated with honors, took white collar jobs, and started repaying $70,000 in student loans. We had followed the system, and we were drowning. It's been 12 years since I graduated college, and I still owe $18,000 dollars on my student loan, and my oldest son has already started college himself. This is the American life??! This is living the dream??

Weary worker, I know you have been there. Your story may be even harder than mine. That's why you have to take this seriously. There is another way.

DREAM JOB

After John and I graduated, I was offered a position with a Christian radio network in upstate New York.

It was a wonderful ministry, but it meant leaving everything we knew behind: our family, our friends, our church, and the doctors who had delivered our babies. It was crazy hard.

But there was the possibility of work for my husband, who had looked for a job for 15 months in Chicago without a single serious offer. And I had prayed for 11 years to work in Christian radio on morning drive so I could be home during the day to homeschool my kids. This was my dream job.

A few nights before Christmas, days before the move from Chicago to upstate New York, I'd tossed my name into a lottery with the Salvation Army. We hadn't had a paycheck in six weeks—and had borrowed from the station for the move. Food was scarce. Christmas wasn't even on the radar. We had just a few dollars in our bank account. That morning, I got a call that our family's name had been chosen in a lottery, and I was to come in and pick out new gifts for our kids.

I walked into that high school gym and saw all the things people had donated — brand new gifts — piled high three-quarters of the way up the gym wall. I was allowed to pick out a new jacket, boots, hats, gloves, a board game, and three presents for each child. I walked out with three 44-gallon garbage bags of the best toys my kids had ever owned and a turkey for Christmas dinner.

I sat in my car with all those new gifts in the backseat and lost it. Twelve years of poverty caught up with me. I wept harder than I ever had: tears of joy at the gifts of strangers, and how they'd made our

Christmas that year; and tears of fear, that I didn't know how long our money famine was going to continue. We worked so hard, yet there we were, with $70,000 in student loans, a car payment, a van payment, credit card debt; and absolutely nothing to show for it at the end of the day but an empty stomach, five little blue-eyed faces trusting us to take care of them, and a government-subsidized townhouse. I was so overwhelmed.

PRAYING LIKE MOSES

That was when I prayed a prayer I'll never forget. I took several minutes and thanked God for every single gift in that car, for the turkey on my front seat, and for all that He had provided. We always had just enough. And we made it because of Him and Him alone. I thanked Him for how He loved us. But then I got bold, and I asked for something more. I asked to be totally rich — beyond my wildest dreams. I asked to make more than I could spend. I prayed for the Moses blessing. Moses waited for 40 days on that mountain to see God, and when He appeared, His glory was so great that Moses was face down on the ground. He never even got to see God. I asked for the blessing to be so great, we couldn't even use it all or see the swath of what the Lord had given.

It wasn't because John and I wanted to own a jet or mansion; it was because every single person we knew lived just like us. There was no way out. There was no hope. For 12 years of our marriage, all we'd done was take from people out of desperation. I was asking the Lord to be the giver. I wanted to be able to give as much as people had given to me, and I couldn't do that when we barely had food. I wanted to live on 10% of my income and give the rest of it away.

Seven years later, God answered that prayer. In 2014, for my 36th birthday, a Young Living premium starter kit showed up on my door. The kit included 11 different bottles of essential oil and a diffuser (which disperses the oils in the air). Essential oils are steam distilled from the plant, and Young Living is a pioneer in distillation. Their methods are copied all over the world. (To learn more, check out seedtoseal.com). Within a week after having our kit, we were able to use essential oils over 80 times successfully. Every oil you use is a chemical you are not using. I wanted to get these in my home in every place that I could: my cleaning supplies, my toothpaste and deodorant, to replace my candles, my supplements; but I could not afford them.

A NEW ADVENTURE

My husband told me if I wanted to get oils every month, I'd have to teach a class and have a few people sign up under me. So without any strategy, without any sales background, I started teaching oils classes. Young Living is a network marketing company. That means as others catch the love of the oils beside you, and start kicking chemicals out of every nook and cranny of their home, your team grows and becomes a snowball rolling down the hill that can lead to financial freedom. I didn't know that at the beginning. All I knew was that I wanted to get the oils for free, and to do that, I had to share what I knew about them.

I grabbed a bunch of aromatherapy encyclopedias and wrote a little 3-page 101 script chronicling all the things I wanted to know about oils: the who, what, when, where, why, and how of essential oils. Then I gathered a few friends to my living room couch and read it. At the end, I pulled out my Young Living starter kit and passed it around so they could smell and experience the oils.

For my first class, on July 18, 2014, I was terrified. I'd done radio for nearly two decades, but that meant staring at a wall six hours a day in a room all by myself. I never had to look at the people I was talking to, so this was a whole new ball game! If you had seen my knees knocking, you would have thought it was comical with my work background. (So don't beat yourself up if you have butterflies! Even famous people that talk to millions of people get them! You're not human if you don't have a little fear!) How did I get through it? I doused myself in Valor essential oil (Stress Away oil works, too), prayed a lot, and just read the script.

After I taught my first class, three people signed up and got their own Young Living premium starter kits! I was in total shock. I didn't think anyone would listen to a word I had to say! Three others who couldn't make it for the class met me for lunch and by the end of the month I was off and running — I had a team of six and was a Young Living Star (that is the first rank in Young Living.) My goal that month was to make $50 and get my oils for free. But my first paycheck ended up being enough to pay my husband back for the starter kit, get business cards, and still have nearly half my check to invest in the business!

MY OWN BUSINESS

As I mentioned earlier, Young Living is a Network Marketing company. If the concept of Network marketing scares the tar out of you — don't let it. The only difference between this and the small business in the downtown of your home town is rental space. They have a brick and mortar store, you educate, and the people that listen buy directly from the farms themselves. There is no middle man. This means there is no product to stock, no website to run, no employees to pay, no franchise fees to cover, no health insurance to pay out of pocket, and no utilities. Young Living handles it all. You just share about the oils.

When you purchase from a large grocery store, you're buying a CEO's third house. When you buy from someone in direct sales, you are putting food on their table, gas in their car, and paying for their little girl's ballet lessons.

And the system works. Les Brown, a former member of the House of Representatives in Ohio, said "network marketing has produced more millionaires than any other single industry in the history of the world." Forbes magazine reports that about 20% of all millionaires globally are working directly for network marketing companies.

If you think it's a scam, think again. I currently have a team of about 3,800 in all 50 states, and 800 of them are actively reading the 3-page script I wrote for my first class to people on their couches every month. More than 100 leaders on my team have retired or semi-retired. They are following a mom with no sales experience, no marketing background, and no network marketing history, who homeschooled five kids and was up every day at 4 a.m. to work a full-time job first. (Most of them are moms and dads, too!) I am thankful every day that I made the decisions I did, even if it was completely by accident, and we now have a guaranteed system for building a successful business with Young Living.

Once I got into the rhythm of my business, I realized pretty fast that I wasn't going to be able to teach during the week, because I was still anchoring news at 4 a.m. every day. A 7 p.m. class was impossible for me because that was my bedtime. So I decided to teach a class Friday night and Saturday morning, then take the next weekend off. That was a commitment of four classes/8 hours a month. I did another two hours of follow-up calls. That second month, my check was enough for my mortgage payment — and my oils!

Eight weeks into my business, I made Executive, the third rank in Young Living. Eighteen days after Executive, I made Silver. In 12 weeks, I had surpassed 16 years of news anchoring income by working less than a quarter of the hours. Five months later, I was Gold. Eight months after that, Platinum! How? By slow, steady classes and a commitment to treat this business as a business, not a hobby.

Sharing that little 3-page script catapulted us to a monthly income that was six times what I was making at the radio station. And it happened within two years. If you can grab those three pages and read them to the people around you, and as we say on my team — rinse and repeat — you will ignite a fire and start your own team. If you are too timid to read it, we even have an audio 101 class (the same three pages) that's completely free to download online at oilabilityteam.com. Share it with the people around you. Then touch base. That's as hard as this gets. That one action, over and over and over again, was the difference between poverty and wealth for our family. It turned our story into a Cinderella story.

RETIRED FROM RADIO

In January, six months after receiving my kit, my husband asked me when I was going to start taking the business seriously, and I told him, "I don't know, Harnisch. You told me to teach oils classes to get my oils for free, so I'm teaching classes, just like you told me!"

But my soft-spoken, gentle-spirited husband replied with, "Are you paying attention? You are making more and working less! I know how much you love it, but it's time to let go of your anchoring job." It took me nine months to get up the courage to step off full-time radio. (I still fill in, just because I love radio so much.) But almost exactly a year after I started Young Living, I was able to retire with no previous network marketing experience. I took a photo of my face the last day I anchored full-time and a photo of my face three weeks later — with eight hours of sleep each night. I look like a totally different person!

Less stress, more family time, better balance in my mommy life.

Please understand, never will I take my years anchoring news for granted. Never do I take the generosity of the radio ministry for granted, or their graciousness in allowing me to step off morning drive and yet still fill in. Never will I take any job for granted, really — no matter where the Lord leads me. But to have such a large prayer answered — I have no answer for that, save the grace of God.

I learned so much in that first year. I made a lot of mistakes. I've been discouraged, and I've been blown away. I've grown and been stretched. I have ten thousand mistakes and ten thousand victories ahead of me. Having a gameplan would have saved me over and over and over again. That is why I put pen to paper; to show you the way out. You have the mini version of my book, Gameplan, in your hands right now, the first two chapters. You can find the full book at OilAbilityTeam.com. It is my story, my strategies, my systems. It is how I ranked. It is how I became free.

I know that each person is unique and has different gifts and talents. I know my road may not be your road, that my pace may not be your pace, and my tactics may not work for you. But I also know there are tools in Gameplan that will save you a lot of time. There are resources that took me quite a while to find, and if I couldn't find them, I wrote them. If I can save you time, you may have a shorter path than I did. One of my life goals is to help every person I possibly can to become financially free. When you are financially free, you have time economy and wealth to invest in the lives of those around you. The best way I can help other people to avoid the life I had is to give them the tools to stand.

Read, be blessed, and teach others what you have learned. Don't let the secrets of this book sit on a shelf. Share it. Give it to a friend who needs inspiration, a friend who is frustrated, stuck, desperate, or who needs a way out. One of the things that makes Young Living so wonderful is that it's about helping other people. You thrive when your team soars. I have had so many people ask me who this book was written for. It's not just for my team or my friends' teams. It's not even just for those in Young Living. It's for anyone who has a dream and wants to see that their dream is possible. Any team, any person, any dream, anywhere.

So take this and fly!

I have just started doing Young Living as a business. Since I began I have seen a whole new me. I have started to balance my life better and feel better. I am becoming a more positive, happier me.

Taylor Phillips

My hesitation to starting Young Living as a business was that I do not do sales. That is not my personality. I had all of the excuses; however, Young Living made such a difference in my life that my lips just could not stay shut! I took the plunge and I brought others with me. And now, my student loans are GONE! I had 12 more years to pay. Yes, I said 12 more years. I paid them in five months. In addition, I have been able to give abundantly to local friends and family in need, as well as to my family of Indian orphans who are building a home and Bible College in India. The only reason I have been able to give is because I said "Yes" to Young Living as a business AND I did not give up. My decision to do Young Living has changed many more lives than my own.

Angela Rhodes Anderson

WHY LAUNCH A YOUNG LIVING BUSINESS?

That's the question I get more than any other. Here's the short answer: it's better than any job you've ever had, including a job you love. (I love anchoring news!) Why?

Freedom.

This is better than what you are doing right now, or you would never have glanced at this book. How you are living right now is not going to get anything crossed off your bucket list in the next five years; but to see that, you have to catch the vision.

I didn't see the business right away. In fact, it took a good six months before my husband finally sat me down and made me take a hard look at my 'hobby.' That's when I realized I needed to take it seriously. The Lord had put something in my path to pull me out of the bondage of my 4 a.m. high-stress anchoring job, and I didn't even see it. It took my husband's wisdom for me to snap out of my routine and my patterns to realize this was a viable job that could really bless our family.

Once I saw it, I made a list of pros to doing my Young Living business based on what I'd seen over our first six months. Was it truly worth it? When I weighed the options, that's when Young Living blew me away. This is that list. This is what I want you to ponder as you head into work tomorrow.

SARAH'S WHY DO A YOUNG LIVING BUSINESS PROS LIST

1. There Is No Income Ceiling

In four months flat, I made more with Young Living than in 16 years of anchoring news. Two years out, I have multiplied the highest monthly income I ever made in my life by six — and the best is yet to come.

If you look at the Income Disclosure Guide in a couple of pages, you'll see the average monthly income for someone ranked Diamond in Young Living is well over what most people usually make in one year. I know people that are living that dream, dozens of them are our close friends. John and I are living that dream. It's possible. The only ones that don't get to the top are the ones that give up.

2. The Timing Has Never Been Better

Many people say that timing is everything, and that you can't be successful in a network marketing company unless you get into the business early. My story and many others disproves that. I didn't get into Young Living until the company was almost 20 years old! Yet, in months I had surpassed nearly every person who got into the business ahead of me, save a handful of people. There are hundreds of Diamonds, hundreds of Platinums, thousands of Golds, and thousands upon thousands of Silvers, and the company continues to experience radical growth even as you read this. It's rare for any network marketing company to cross the one billion dollar threshold in sales. Young Living has done it. Most network marketing companies fail within seven years. Young Living has been around three times that long, because the oils work.

The date that you sign up for Young Living has no bearing on where this business will go for you. How do I know? Because the current market has never been more open to what you have to offer. In just the past five years, Panera Bread has cut all chemicals from their salad dressings. Kraft Mac and Cheese has cut all dyes from their sauce. Chipotle has vowed to cut all GMOs from their menu. People are demanding better food and better products. You're seeing more and more items on store shelves that are "simple" or "natural" versions — peanut butter with peanuts and salt instead of hydrogenated oils and soy products. And the stuff is selling.

This world has started to dramatically change. No longer do we accept at face value that everything in a store is safe simply because it made it past the government. We are starting to flip over the bottles and boxes of the foods that we consume and the things we use to clean our home, and the personal care products we use to scrub our teeth and slather on our armpits and say, "I think there's a better way to do this." The companies that are keeping up with that trend are thriving. Those that don't will lose. Young Living is ahead of the game in every single field: oils, personal care, cleaning supplies, supplements, and more. They are a total wellness company. Wellness means you stay above the line of disease.

Do you ever get frustrated that it seems doctors are always treating the symptoms instead of the cause? That they chase inflammation, pain, headaches, and a plethora of other ailments instead of finding out what's underneath all that and stopping it? You're not alone.

That's what Young Living is about. It's about stopping the cause before it happens by supporting all the systems in your body without chemically overloading them. It's not about treating disease, it's about staying ahead of it: preventative maintenance.

The average woman applies eighty chemicals to her body daily before breakfast through four types of products: makeup, hair care, skin care, and soap. And we wonder why our livers are taxed and we are tired and have hormonal issues! It's the yuck in our life. We are in constant chemical exhaustion.

This means that if you meet any person who has not banned that stuff from the threshold of their doors, any person who is not label-reading every product in their home — you have just found a potential oiler. You have a market that is one hundred percent wide open, because literally every person you know needs oils. It's not like a pan, or lipstick, or a book, or a skirt. It's about your health. It's about your life and your family's lives. That's what makes this company the best.

I believe with all my heart that Young Living will continue to absolutely boom — because they have what everyone wants: health freedom. It is what wellness is all about, getting ahead of your health by saying "no" to the things you allow across the threshold of the door to your home. You are the gatekeeper. And if you teach others to be a gatekeeper, you have the secret to unlocking an explosive business with unlimited customers.

3. You Are Your Own Boss and Set Your Own Hours

I had no idea how much I appreciated this until I had no boss! I dictate my own schedule every single day. And to a weary momma who has been getting up hours before the sun rises for years, you can't put a price tag on that.

One of my best moments was a few days after I retired. I woke up to the sun in my face, and stumbled out into the living room to watch the sun rise over the fields behind our home. I had not seen the sun rise in nearly ten years. I had my weekends off, but from sheer exhaustion, I always slept well past the sun coming up. Now, I get to be home with my kids and see the sun rise every day. Some of the smallest things bring the greatest joy. To me, a sunrise means freedom.

4. Willable Income (The Best Perk Ever!)

Once you make $3,000 a month and write a personal will, then connect with Young Living and fill out their paperwork; the income your business generates will go to your spouse and kids forever. So, say you have five kids (like me), and are making $15,000 a month as a Platinum—that's $3,000 a month for each child! My kids will never grow up without food in their stomach or a roof over their head. Young Living brings peace of mind. That's the biggest perk to me. It's a legacy income, not a 401K that disappears when the cash is gone.

Outside of network marketing, there is no job on the earth where you can pull that off. If I passed away while working in radio, two weeks after my death, my final news anchor check would show up. My family would be out of luck. The $17,000 I saved in my 401K over nine years would be gone in about six months. A Young Living business doesn't work like that. This isn't some account somewhere with cash in it; it's a real, living, growing business that generates capitol — cash that goes to your family every single month.

Young Living is like setting up a storefront in your hometown and having employees run it for you. It keeps generating income even after you're gone. If you have a will, your rank in the Young Living hierarchy doesn't disappear after your death; it goes to your family.

5. You Can Take Time Off—and Still Get Paid!

If you were in a car accident tomorrow and missed three months of work, your paycheck at a regular job would drop off within a few weeks, right? Even with disability insurance, it would be a fraction of what it usually is. But with network marketing, if you are in a season where you can't share the oils, the powerful team beneath you is still working.

This was one of my wow moments, where I really grasped the power of network marketing for the first time. John and I have a special needs son on the autism spectrum. When he was 14, we had to have him placed in a school on the other side of the country. We had homeschooled all five of our kids together for 12 years, and it was extremely painful to split the Harnisch herd up. Gabe was at that school for an entire year. For 12 months, save a visit at Christmas, we did not see him, and had to get by with a 20-minute weekly phone call. At Christmas the next year, he came home. It was a huge milestone for our family. We had missed him terribly!!

These are our two oldest sons, minutes after Isaiah saw his older brother.

When Gabe returned, I felt convicted that all of my time needed to be spent on assimilating him back into the family. So I committed to take 30 straight days off from Young Living: no phone calls, no training, no classes, not even Facebook posts. I put all my attention on him, and reintegrating him into the house and our routines. From December 6 until January 9, 2015, I didn't do a thing for my business. I figured it would be a period of famine for us that year, but it was more important to focus on Gabe than on work. We'd just have to get through.

But four days before Christmas, I got a Young Living check in the mail that was higher than my monthly income from my full-time job. I scratched my head, took it to John, and told him, "I didn't do anything this month!" I hadn't anchored news either, so there was no paycheck from the radio station. I had only been doing Young Living for five months and hadn't even taught any classes in December, but I still got paid because the team underneath me was out there selling. This was the power of network marketing at work for our family! When I was at my low point, my team (and my paycheck) were still there!

I tell you, I came back more excited than ever, and started a firestorm of teaching after January 9th when Gabe was comfortable at home and had enrolled in college. That firestorm led us to Gold rank just twelve weeks after his return.

There will be seasons in your life that make it tough to do Young Living well. It's okay. When the season passes, keep going. In the interim, you have the strength of the team under you. It's the best structure of any job there is.

6. Relationships: The Surprise Benefit

I had no idea how small my circle of friends was until I got involved in network marketing. You get into a groove with a nine-to-five job, or homeschooling, or public schooling, or running your home, and simply forget that the Lord created us for relationships and that we thrive when we're in community. Some of us need many, many friends, while others are fine with just a couple of them. But we all need to take time to connect with the women and men that inspire us and make us better people.

Until two years ago, I had very little contact with the outside world, save trivial relationships, because I was either news anchoring or home-schooling. That has completely changed for me now because of Young Living. In 24 months, I have a team of over 3,800 in all 50 states and several countries and have developed some serious relationships that I know will last my lifetime. Hundreds of them would drop everything and open their home to me in an emergency. I look forward to my girl time at our Oil Ability Silver Retreats and our adventures at the Young Living convention. Even outside of my own team, I have true friendships around the entire world. We grow and laugh and make memories together each time we see one other.

There are members on my team that run their business for the sole reason of developing deeper relationships. And that's a great "why." Young Living has an incredible way of networking us with people when we need to be poured into, and allows us to be a spigot to pour into others. This is an aspect of the business that I completely underestimated that has blessed me more than I can put on paper.

7. Guaranteed Bonuses

Young Living is a generous company that has built-in bonuses and perks for every level in the business. If you do the work, you will be rewarded. The ranks in Young Living are Star, Senior Star, Executive, Silver, Gold, Platinum, Diamond, Crown Diamond, and Royal Crown Diamond. Each rank has perks and bonuses!

Stars, Senior Stars, and Executives get increasingly bigger paychecks.

Anyone who holds Silver rank goes to the largest essential oils farm in the world, Young Living at Mona, Utah, for three days. The company pays to fly you there, puts you up in a posh resort, loves on you with a swag bag worth a few hundred dollars, and feeds you like a king. You'll make friends from around the world and catch the vision of where Young Living goes.

Golds get the same thing, but this time they travel to the first Young Living farm in Saint Maries, Idaho.

Platinums head to the farm in Ecuador and see Ylang Ylang, Dorado Azul, and Copaiba, and witness the work of the Young Living Foundation (learn more at younglivingfoundation.org). The foundation is responsible for many projects, but one that I got to see first-hand was a 200 million dollar school for impoverished kids that they built in Ecuador.

Not only do you get to see the work they are doing, you get to be a part of it. In one afternoon, a team of Platinums and I walked into a room full of books and turned it into a working library for 300 kids at the school. It's change you can be a part of.

Gary Young is the founder of Young Living. Each day as he drove to the Young Living farm in Ecuador, he passed a small schoolhouse with no bathroom where 60 kids had classes. Gary received no financial benefit from building a school for hundreds of kids in a tiny town in Ecuador, but he did it anyway. It's part of the purpose of the entire company — to make a difference.

The motto of Young Living is wellness, purpose, and abundance. When they say purpose, they mean it. It was one of the greatest moments in all of my time in Young Living, to see those kids up close, talk to them, build a library in their school for them, and know that none of it would exist without the generosity of a Young Living oils farm a few miles down the road. Do you know what a blessing it is that each time I sit and speak to someone about oils, share that simple 3-page script, and show them how to get away from chemical living; that some of the profits from that starter kit goes to projects like this? You can make a difference. Even while running your family business from a couch.

Diamond retreats are in different locations around the globe each year. They get new products before they are released, front row seating at convention, and are paid a hefty Diamond bonus every month for attending the Diamond retreat or convention. Young Living wants their

As a direct selling company selling essential oils, supplements, and other lifestyle products, Your
on our products.

Whatever your interest in the company, we hope to count you among the more than 1 million Yo
home in the world.

What are my earning opportunities?

Members can earn commissions and bonuses as outlined in our Compensation Plan. As membe
opportunities.

This document provides statistical, fiscal data about the average member income, average hour:

RANK	AVERAGE HOURS WORKED PER WEEK[2]	PERCENTAGE OF ALL MEMBERS[3]	Lowest
Distributor	3	93.1%	$0
Star	8	4.4%	$0
Senior Star	9	1.5%	$0
Executive	11	0.6%	$0
Silver	18	0.3%	$306
Gold	24	0.1%	$1,952
Platinum	33	< 0.1%	$5,064
Diamond	31	< 0.1%	$13,871
Crown Diamond	39	< 0.1%	$31,693
Royal Crown Diamond	37	< 0.1%	$53,723

The income statistics in this statement are for incomes earned7 by all active worldwide members
12 months.8 The average annual income for all members in this time period was $28, and the me
in 2014 and 54 percent of all members who enrolled in 2013 did not remain active members with

Please note that compensation paid to members summarized in this disclosure does not include
which can vary widely and might include advertising or promotional expenses, product samples,
members in this chart are not necessarily representative of the income, if any, that a Young Living
not be considered as guarantees or projections of your actual earnings or profits. Your success w
Young Living does not guarantee any income or rank success.

[1] Based on a count at the end of December 2015.
[2] Based on a survey of Young Living members in December 2015.
[3] Because a member's rank may change during the year, these percentages are not based on individual member ranks throu
[4] Because a member's rank may change during the year, these incomes are not based on individual member incomes throug
the year.
[5] This is calculated by multiplying the average monthly income by 12.
[6] These statistics include all historical ranking data for each rank and are not limited to members who achieved these ranks in

INCOME DISCLOSURE STATEMENT

ing Living offers opportunities for our members to build a business or simply receive discounts

oung Living members joining us in our mission to bring Young Living essential oils to every

ers move up in the ranks of Young Living, they become eligible for additional earning

rs worked per week, and information about achieving various ranks.

MONTHLY INCOME[4]			ANNUALIZE AVERAGE INCOME[5]	MONTHS TO ACHIEVE THIS RANK[6]		
Highest	Median	Average		Low	Average	High
$3,643	$0	$1	$12	N/A	N/A	N/A
$834	$59	$79	$948	1	12	240
$7,089	$208	$255	$3,060	1	18	239
$12,404	$463	$549	$6,492	1	23	233
$27,826	$1,769	$2,221	$26,652	1	32	228
$39,655	$4,879	$6,042	$72,504	1	53	239
$57,606	$12,043	$14,710	$176,520	2	63	238
$144,369	$29,846	$38,750	$465,000	10	83	221
$204,917	$63,624	$74,335	$892,020	14	91	236
$241,324	$144,985	$141,851	$1,702,212	17	126	230

rs in 2015. An "active" member is a member who has purchased at least 50 PV in the previous
nedian annual income for all members was $0. Forty-two percent of all members who enrolled
h Young Living in 2015.

e expenses incurred by a member in the operation or promotion of his or her business,
s, training, rent, travel, telephone, Internet, and miscellaneous expenses. The earnings of the
ng member can or will earn through the Young Living Compensation Plan. These figures should
will depend on individual diligence, work, effort, sales skill, and market conditions.

ughout the entire year. They are based on the average distribution of member ranks during the entire year.
ughout the entire year. They are based on earnings of all members qualifying for each rank during any month throughout

in 2015.

top leaders there and gives generously to have them come. They also get regular conference calls from Young Living to get the latest inside information from the company (which is my favorite Diamond perk!).

And if none of those reasons rock your world, how about this one: you can earn a ridiculous paycheck!! Check out the 2015 income disclosure guide. These are average incomes from all Young Living distributors!

8. Financial freedom

Young Living is a vehicle to financial freedom. But it's about so much more than the money. Let me explain.

Not only are my husband and I nearly debt free (including $70,000 in student loans), but I have had the honor of watching many of my closest friends and family members do the same thing with their Young Living paycheck. If you're going to get rich, do it beside your friends and family! It's been incredible to watch friends pay cash for their wedding, watch my mom buy a home, see my downline members invest in missions, become debt free, give to the needy, let jobs go and stay home with their kids, retire their spouses, go on family vacations before their teens leave for college, cross things off their lifelong bucket lists, travel, and chase their dreams.

Many of my friends have asked me if Young Living is a prosperity gospel or a get-rich-quick scheme. No, it's not. If you think it's a get-rich-quick scheme, you're making the assumption that a Young Living business is handed to you. Let me tell you, you will work and you will work hard! If anyone tells you otherwise, you're being fed a lie. There is no outstretching of your hands and waiting for the cash to fall from the sky. Sometimes it's difficult. People won't come to your classes. Leaders will drive you batty. But my worst day in Young Living has been better than my best day at forty other jobs I've held.

Are you willing to stick it out and see where it goes? Do you have the tenacity to pull this off? If you look at that Young Living Income Disclosure chart—and truly believe where it goes—isn't it worth the push to keep going? Heck, I would work at a Dollar Store for ten years if I knew I could make $30,000 a month eventually! That's what this is. No other job I've ever worked has had a chart like that. It's raw truth. Those are the stats. That's where people land when they push through the tough times. Stick it out and create your dream! Keep fighting and never give up. Some will make it to Diamond in two years, and some in twenty years. But Diamond is Diamond. And it's worth every no, every no-show, and every dissident leader. Don't give up too soon! Be so busy teaching classes that you don't have time to notice the no's.

So many people are afraid of abundance. I scratch my head on that one! When the Lord gives you more, it means you are able to give more. It means you've been trusted with wealth. Some of God's favorite people were wealthy: David, Solomon, Abraham, and Job. Wealth is a blessing that gives you time, peace of mind, resources, and the ability to love more generously on others. I am really enjoying this season of giving when I see a need, and knowing I'll still be able to put dinner on my table that night. There is something beautiful in coming beside someone hurting or in financial pain and making a difference, even anonymously. That is waiting for you with this business: the ability to silently bless.

YOU CAN'T FREE OTHERS WHEN YOU'RE IN BONDAGE

God wants abundance for His people. How are you supposed to take care of the widows, the sick, and the poor when you have a blown head gasket on your car, $100 in your account, and are short for your electric bill this month?

We love Dave Ramsey's financial advice and have taken Financial Peace University. He says to save $1,000, make a list of all your debts from the smallest to largest, and start paying them off, beginning with the smallest debt first. We had done that so many times. But the reality is that when you and your husband are working four minimum wage, full-time jobs just to make ends meet, you just don't have the income to pull it off. We'd save that thousand, then blow the transmission in our car. We'd save it again, then the water heater would go out in our home. We found that we could never, ever get ahead, and that's how we lived for nearly two decades. Save it, lose it. Save it, lose it. How can you help others when you are in that place?

That is why we are here — to serve. You can't serve when you can't stand. John and I were technically middle class, but we were drowning. We are not drowning any more, and we will never drown again. We live by Dave Ramsey now and can actually do his debt reduction strategy, because the crisis period in our lives has ended. Even as a middle class family in the richest nation on earth, we could not breathe with our regular jobs. You'll hear me say it so many times in this book: Young Living is a way out. The Lord has sent you a boat. Get on it and get off that island where you're financially stranded.

IT'S NOT ABOUT FAME AND FORTUNE

As a radio anchor I've had my name in millions of homes, so I know what it's like to be famous. I've had my name and face on many a banner and billboard. As a Platinum in Young Living I've received recognition, been on stage, and traveled the world. But I'll tell you, freedom is better than being famous. Why? Because I can be home with my kids. I have time to take care of my husband and take care of my body. I have the ability to run with my teenagers in the woods in the morning and stay up late watching their soccer games and talking into the night about their relationships and their faith, without having to rise at 4 a.m. to anchor news. I have the ability to wake up and have a candlelight breakfast with my husband and do devotions without interruption. I have the ability to give, and that drives me. I have the ability to see others set free — especially struggling families. Those are my "why's."

Money Doesn't Drive Me. Freedom Does.

I share Young Living to break the cycle of poverty where I see so many families living. How can you do what you were called and created to do when you're constantly in survival mode? You can't. And that is where the business comes in. That little ripple in the pond of my oils business became a tsunami throughout New York and Pennsylvania, and I started seeing something I didn't expect to see as I got out there and taught. People weren't just experiencing wellness — they were becoming financially free!

First it was a mom on my team, able to stop working and stay home with her children.

Then my own mom's check surpassed her full time job.

Then a Silver on my team, married to a legally blind husband, was able to quit her $10/hour desk job that she'd had at different offices for 15 years.

Then my own sister, who had worked three jobs for 20 years, retired from one job, then two, then a month before her wedding, retired from her third and final job.

One by one, people were seeing freedom. At the beginning, it was just a few people sharing the oils. Then in 18 months, we had 800 leaders. One in every five people on my team were sharing. Most were just getting their oils for free, but many were able to make game-changer decisions with their life: retire themselves, retire their spouse, or pay off copious amounts of debt.

At the time of publishing this book, dozens of leaders on our team have either cut back or fully retired from their jobs. Those families have been forever changed because of a freak news-anchor homeschooling mom of five who was exhausted, living in a rural area, and thought she couldn't make a difference for anyone.

RAISING DIAMONDS

Now, my "why" is to raise as many Diamonds as I can. If you are on my team, that's a blessing, because you may be a close friend or a family member and I have the honor of getting to watch amazing things happen in your life. But if you are not on my team, that's part of my purpose too. You matter. It's because Young Living isn't just about me or my family. I got outside that circle with my very first class. It's about abundance, wellness, and purpose.

Abundance means you're financially free and have the time economy to do the things the Lord has called and created you to do. How do you do that when you are tied down at a 40-hour/week job and have nothing in the bank? That's not freedom. That's slavery. I am no longer a slave!

Wellness means you are educated on the product and living a life where you make conscious choices to take care of yourself.

Purpose means you take that healthy self of yours and pour into the people around you with the same passion that was poured into you. Keep the spark going. Show others how to be free. You are a hope-bringer. You are a path-changer. You were born for Diamond.

My goal with Gameplan is to show you how to get your own freedom. I'm here to train you how to start that ripple in your pond, and then how to fight for it. I want to see as many Diamonds packed onto that Young Living stage as possible.

IT'S TIME TO START

Remember the Income Disclosure Chart earlier in this chapter? John and I are Platinums on that chart! Crazy, huh?? And it happened in 17 months. This is doable. You just have to understand the strategy of how to pull it off. And that's what my book, Gameplan, is about. The full version of the Gameplan book (26 chapters and 13 Appendixes loaded with scripts) is a meat and potatoes, get-from-point-A-to-point-B book.

You can read it, re-read it, highlight it and make your own personal game plan by filling in the Gameplan workbook. You can get Gameplan books (at oilabilityteam.com) for your friends and get them on the same page. You can use the scripts in the back of the Gameplan book to rock this business. You will not have to figure things out on your own. You will have a guide. Gameplan will fill your head with ideas and you will see network marketing from a different, doable perspective.

That's what Gameplan is — thousands of hours of study, trial and error in our own business and fool-proof tips that work, all in an easy-to-understand format. You'll find tips on how to fill classes, how to do this if you're shy, how to find new friend circles, how to do follow up, and how to raise leaders. All of it is in one simple place. You don't need ten books to learn how to start this trade. Just one. Gameplan.

The only thing that is uncertain is your commitment and dedication to see it through. The neat thing is that you are the one who controls commitment. You control your ability to dig out. So share the oils with people! A few will get a kit. Share again. A few more will get a kit. Share again the same month and follow up with the first few you talked with, and you'll have more people on your team and even a few who will share the oils with others. It grows and grows. Mentally prepare yourself for the abundance that's coming, and brace yourself for what's ahead!

You were made to be free. So call it out, speak life over yourself, and run! It's time to move. The place you are now is not giving you the results you're looking for. Your bucket list will remain unchanged in five years if you don't regroup, refocus, and make a gameplan. You are the only one with the power to alter the outcome.

This is your year to get your game on.

WHAT'S NEXT?

You did it. You made it! You have survived "Your Gameplan," a mini version of the full Gameplan book. There are far too many success stories from this system for you to ignore this. I am begging you to continue moving forward. From me, a woman who battled poverty for almost four decades — speaking directly to you... don't give up before you start.

YOUR NEXT MOVE

Contact the person that gave you this book. (Their information is right at the back of this book). They have poured into you. They compassionately got this for you and put it in your hands to offer you hope. Reciprocate and ask them how to begin. Ask them to be trained. They will walk you through a simple 3-page teacher training. They will coach you through your first class—even if you're just reading that 101 Script in front of your mom and best friend. When you get through it, you're ready for the full Gameplan book and workbook. If you're Ninja Warrior tough, there's even a free video bootcamp that walks you through every single chapter of the full Gameplan book, piece by piece. I shot every video myself. I am talking directly to you, motivating and training you. You can find the videos under "Gameplan Bootcamp" at oilabilityteam. com.

Here's the thing — you can do this. I know you can. You were not made to be caged. You were created to serve and to love and to pour into those around you. But you can't do it when your spigot has run dry. It's time for you to move. Take a moment and make a list of the things that you struggle with at your current job. Then next to that list, make a list of the eight perks in Young Living. Seriously consider and weigh the two side by side. I believe you will see that Young Living is the better choice.

Are the ways you are spending your time right now getting you to the places you want to be? If not, it's time to re-evaluate. It's time to start something new. It's time for a Gameplan.

My Job	Young Living
1	1
2	2
3	3
4	4
5	5
6	6
7	7
8	8